# Adjectives

*for fiction writers*

Mary Ellis

#  A

**able**
intelligent, clever,
brilliant, talented,
skilled, accomplished,
gifted

**above**
previous, former,
prior

**abrupt**
sudden, immediate,
instantaneous,
hurried, hasty,
quick, swift, rapid,
speedy

**absolute**
complete, total,
utter, outright,
entire, perfect, pure

**absurd**
ridiculous, ludicrous

**acceptable**
satisfactory,
adequate,
reasonable, fair,
decent, sufficient,
fine

**accurate**
correct, precise,
exact, right, perfect,
valid, specific,
detailed

**acid**
sour, bitter, sharp,
biting, acrid,
pungent

**acrid**
pungent, bitter,
sharp, sour, harsh,
acid

**active**
working, functional,
operational, live

**actual**
real, true, genuine,
authentic, definite,
hard, plain, clear

**acute**
keen, sharp, good,
penetrating,
perceptive, sensitive,
subtle

**additional**
extra, added,
secondary

**adjunct**
additional, extra,
backup, spare, other

**adult**

mature, grown-up

**advanced**
state-of-the-art,
new, modern

**afraid**
frightened, scared,
fearful, nervous

**aggressive**
hostile, belligerent

**aghast**
amazed, dismayed,
stunned, shocked,
shell-shocked,
staggered

**alarming**
frightening,
startling, unnerving,
shocking

**alert**
vigilant, aware,
watchful, attentive,
wary

**alien**
foreign, external,
distant, remote

**alone**
solo, lone, solitary,
single

**amazing**
astonishing,
surprising, stunning,
staggering, shocking,
startling,
breathtaking

**ambitious**
determined,
forceful, pushy,
eager, enthusiastic,
energetic

**ample**
enough, sufficient,
adequate

**amusing**
entertaining, funny,
comical, humorous,
witty, hilarious,
ludicrous

**ancient**
first, early, past,
former

**angry**
annoyed, irritated,
indignant

**annoyed**
irritated, angry,
disgruntled

**anonymous**
unnamed, nameless,
unidentified,
unknown

**anxious**

worried, concerned,
apprehensive,
fearful, uneasy,
troubled, disturbed,
distressed

**apologetic**
regretful, sorry,
contrite, rueful

**apparent**
evident, plain,
obvious, clear,
visible, discernible,
perceptible,
noticeable,
recognizable

**appropriate**
suitable, proper,
fitting, apt

**apt**
suitable, fitting,
appropriate,
relevant, fit

**arrogant**
haughty, superior

**artificial**
synthetic, fake, false,
mock

**ashamed**
sorry, sheepish,
guilty, contrite

**asleep**
resting, dormant

**astonishing**
amazing, staggering,
shocking, surprising,
breathtaking,
striking, impressive,
stunning

**athletic**
muscular, sturdy,
strong, powerful,
robust, vigorous

**attractive**
appealing, agreeable,
pleasing, tempting,
interesting,
fascinating,
irresistible

**audible**
perceptible,
discernible,
recognizable

**average**
mean, middle

**awake**
sleepless, conscious

**awesome**
breathtaking,
amazing, stunning,
astonishing,
staggering,
extraordinary,

incredible,
unbelievable
**awful**
disgusting, nasty,
terrible, dreadful,
ghastly, horrid,
horrible, vile, foul,
appalling
**awkward**
difficult, tricky

# B

**bad**
poor, inferior, inadequate, unacceptable

**baggy**
loose-fitting, loose, full, ample, voluminous

**bald**
hairless, smooth

**barbed**
jagged, hooked, spiky, spiked, prickly, thorny, scratchy

**bare**
naked, exposed

**barren**
sterile, desolate

**basic**
fundamental, rudimentary, primary, principal, chief, elementary, elemental

**beautiful**
attractive, pretty, handsome, good-looking, pleasing

**beloved**
dear, precious, favorite, cherished, prized

**bent**
twisted, crooked, contorted, misshapen, irregular

**big**
large, substantial, considerable, great, huge, immense, enormous, extensive, colossal, massive

**bitter**
sharp, acid, pungent, acrid, sour, biting, harsh

**bizarre**
strange, peculiar, odd, funny, curious, eccentric, unconventional, queer, unexpected

**black**
dark, pitch-black, jet-black, inky

**bland**
mild, weak, thin, watery

**blank**
empty, unmarked, unused, clear, free, bare, clean, plain, spotless, white

**bleak**
bare, exposed, desolate, stark, open, empty, windswept

**blind**
sightless, unseeing

**blonde**
fair, light, yellow, yellowish, golden, silver, silvery

**bloody**
damn, damned, flaming, precious, rotten, wretched

**blue**
sky-blue, sapphire

**blunt**
dull, worn

**bold**
daring, courageous, brave, valiant, fearless, unafraid, undaunted

**bony**
gaunt, angular, skinny, thin, lean, spare, skeletal

**booming**
resounding, thundering, thunderous

**boring**
tedious, dull, monotonous

**brave**
courageous, fearless, valiant, heroic, bold, daring

**brief**
short, crisp

**bright**
light, brilliant, vivid, dazzling, beaming, intense, glaring

**brilliant**
gifted, talented, accomplished, ingenious, creative

**brisk**
quick, rapid, fast, swift, speedy

**brittle**

fragile, frail, delicate

**broad**
wide, large, big

**bronze**
chestnut, tan

**brutal**
savage, cruel, bloodthirsty, vicious, ferocious, barbaric, wicked, murderous, cold-blooded, harsh

**bulky**
large, big, great, huge, substantial, voluminous, immense, enormous, colossal

**burly**
sturdy, broad-shouldered, strong, muscular, athletic

# C

**calm**
serene, tranquil,
unruffled,
undisturbed,
unmoved

**capable**
competent, able,
efficient, effective,
accomplished,
adept, apt,
experienced

**careful**
cautious, alert,
aware, attentive,
watchful, vigilant,
wary, prudent

**casual**
indifferent,
unconcerned

**cautious**
careful, wary, aware,
attentive, alert,
watchful, vigilant,
prudent, guarded

**cavernous**
vast, huge, large,
immense, spacious,
airy, voluminous,
ample

**central**
middle, halfway,
mean

**ceremonial**
formal, official,
public

**certain**
sure, confident,
positive, convinced,
satisfied

**charming**
delightful, pleasing,
pleasant, agreeable,
lovely, adorable,
cute, sweet,
appealing

**cheap**
economic,
competitive,
reasonable

**cheerful**
happy, jolly, merry,
bright, glad, sunny,
joyful, joyous,
sparkling

**cheery**
jolly, happy, merry,
bright, cheerful,

glad, sunny, joyful,
joyous, sparkling

**chief**
principal, foremost,
supreme, grand,
superior

**chill**
cold, chilly, cool,
crisp, fresh, brisk

**chilly**
cold, cool, crisp,
fresh, brisk, bleak,
wintry, snowy,
frosty, icy, ice-cold

**civilized**
polite, courteous,
civil, gracious

**clammy**
moist, damp,
sweaty, sticky

**classic**
definitive,
authoritative

**clear**
understandable,
plain, direct,
uncomplicated,
explicit, lucid,
coherent, logical

**clever**

intelligent, bright,
smart, brilliant

**close**
near, adjacent

**closed**
waterproof, tight,
sealed

**cloudy**
overcast, clouded

**clumsy**
awkward, ungainly,
lumbering

**coarse**
rough, scratchy,
prickly, hairy,
shaggy, wiry

**cocky**
arrogant, smug,
haughty, lofty,
proud

**coincidental**
accidental, casual,
random

**cold**
chilly, cool, icy,
snowy, wintry, crisp,
frosty, frigid, bitter

**collective**
common, shared,
joint, combined,

mutual, communal,
allied, cooperative

**comfortable**
pleasant, luxurious,
gracious, opulent,
elegant

**comforting**
sympathetic,
compassionate,
gentle, tender,
warm, protective

**comic**
humorous, funny,
amusing,
entertaining,
absurd, ridiculous,
comical, silly

**commanding**
dominant, superior,
powerful,
prominent,
preferable

**common**
ordinary, normal,
typical, average,
plain, simple

**compelling**
gripping, hypnotic

**competent**
capable, able, adept,
accomplished,

skilled, gifted,
talented

**complete**
entire, whole, full,
total, intact

**complex**
complicated,
involved, intricate,
tangled, elaborate,
serpentine,
impenetrable

**complicated**
complex, intricate,
involved, tangled,
elaborate,
impenetrable,
tricky, thorny,
serpentine

**concerned**
worried, anxious,
disturbed, troubled,
distressed, upset,
uneasy,
apprehensive

**concrete**
solid, real, physical,
tangible, palpable,
visible, existing

**confident**
optimistic, hopeful

**confidential**

private, personal,
intimate, privileged,
quiet

**confusing**
difficult, unclear,
puzzling, mysterious

**conscious**
aware, awake, alert,
sentient

**considerable**
substantial,
significant

**consistent**
steady, stable,
constant, regular,
even, uniform,
orderly

**constant**
continuous,
persistent

**content**
contented, satisfied,
pleased

**convenient**
suitable,
appropriate, fitting,
fit, agreeable

**convinced**
certain, sure,
confident, satisfied

**convincing**

persuasive,
powerful, potent,
strong, forceful,
compelling,
irresistible

**cool**
chilly, cold

**corporate**
collective, shared,
common,
communal, joint,
combined, allied

**correct**
right, accurate, true,
exact, precise,
faithful, strict,
flawless

**countless**
innumerable,
untold, numerous

**cracked**
broken, fractured

**crazed**
mad, insane, lunatic,
wild, distraught,
manic

**crazy**
mad, insane, crazed,
lunatic, unstable

**creamy**

smooth, thick, velvety, rich

**creative**
experimental, original

**creepy**
frightening, terrifying, chilling, alarming, shocking

**criminal**
illegal, illicit, illegitimate

**crimson**
red, reddish, scarlet, bloodred, pink

**crooked**
sinuous, serpentine, irregular

**crowded**
packed, crushed, cramped, full

**crucial**
critical, key, decisive

**cruel**
brutal, savage, inhuman, barbaric, bloodthirsty, murderous, vicious, ferocious

**crying**
tearful, weeping

**cunning**
crafty, devious, sly, tricky, slippery, slick

**curious**
inquisitive, interested

**curly**
wavy, kinky, fuzzy

**current**
contemporary, present, ongoing

**curt**
terse, brusque, abrupt, blunt, short, sharp, crisp

**customary**
usual, traditional, normal, conventional

**cute**
adorable, sweet, lovely, appealing, delightful, dear, winning

# D

**daily**
everyday, day-to-day

**damned**
cursed, accursed,
doomed, lost

**dangerous**
threatening,
treacherous

**dank**
damp, musty, chilly,
clammy, wet, moist,
humid

**daring**
bold, adventurous,
fearless, brave,
unafraid,
undaunted, valiant

**dark**
black, pitch-black,
inky, jet-black

**dazzling**
glaring, brilliant

**deadly**
fatal, lethal, mortal

**dear**
beloved, cherished,
precious

**decent**
proper, correct,
appropriate, apt,
fitting, fit, right,
suitable, respectable,
dignified

**defiant**
resistant,
challenging

**definite**
explicit, specific,
express, precise,
exact

**deliberate**
intentional,
calculated,
conscious, intended,
planned, wanton

**delicate**
fine, exquisite,
intricate, dainty,
airy, elegant,
graceful

**delighted**
glad, happy, joyful,
ecstatic, blissful

**demonic**
satanic, hellish,
infernal, evil, wicked

**dense**

thick, packed,
crowded, compact

**desolate**
barren, bleak, stark,
bare, dismal, grim

**destructive**
devastating,
disastrous,
catastrophic

**detailed**
full, complete,
circumstantial,
thorough

**devastating**
destructive,
disastrous,
catastrophic

**difficult**
hard, arduous,
heavy, tough,
demanding

**dim**
faint, weak, feeble,
soft, pale, dull,
dingy, subdued,
muted, flat

**dire**
terrible, dreadful,
appalling, awful,
horrible, grim,

unspeakable,
alarming

**dirty**
grimy, grubby,
filthy, unwashed,
greasy, spotted

**disappointed**
upset, downcast,
depressed, dismayed

**disastrous**
catastrophic, tragic

**discreet**
careful, cautious,
wary, guarded

**disgusting**
repulsive, sickening,
nauseous

**dismissive**
contemptuous,
negative,
perfunctory

**distant**
faraway, far

**distinct**
separate, individual,
different, detached

**distinctive**
characteristic,
typical, individual,
particular, peculiar,

unique, exclusive,
special

**distraught**
worried, upset,
distressed, fraught,
devastated,
shattered

**distressed**
devastated, crushed,
shattered, desolate

**dizzy**
giddy, light-headed,
faint, weak,
unsteady, shaky,
wobbly, off-balance

**double**
dual, twin

**doubtful**
hesitant, tentative

**dreadful**
terrible, horrible,
grim, awful, dire

**drunk**
drunken, incapable

**drunken**
drunk, incapable

**dry**
parched, burned,
hot, sizzling

**dubious**

doubtful, uncertain,
unsure, hesitant

**dull**
boring, tedious,
tiresome, dry, flat,
bland, featureless

**dumb**
speechless, wordless,
silent, tight-lipped

**dusty**
dirty, grimy, grubby

# E

**eager**
keen, enthusiastic, avid, fervent, passionate, dedicated, committed

**early**
forward, prior

**earnest**
serious, solemn, grave, sober, steady, intense

**easy**
uncomplicated, effortless, painless, simple, straightforward, elementary

**eerie**
uncanny, sinister, ghostly, spectral, unnatural, unearthly, preternatural, supernatural, unreal, mysterious, strange

**effective**
successful, productive, functional, potent, powerful

**efficient**
methodical, logical, coherent, orderly, businesslike

**elaborate**
complicated, detailed, intricate, complex, involved, serpentine, tangled, confusing

**elderly**
old, mature, senior, ancient

**eldest**
first, big

**electronic**
mechanical, automated, computerized, robotic

**elegant**
stylish, graceful, refined, sophisticated, dignified, distinguished,

classic, smart,
fashionable

**embarrassed**
awkward, self-conscious, uneasy,
uncomfortable,
unsettled, sheepish,
red-faced, shy

**emotional**
spiritual, inner,
psychic,
psychological

**empty**
vacant, unoccupied,
clear, free, bare,
desolate, abandoned

**endless**
unlimited, limitless,
infinite, untold

**enormous**
huge, vast, extensive,
expansive, broad,
wide

**enthusiastic**
eager, keen, avid,
fervent, warm,
passionate, lively,
energetic, vigorous

**entire**
whole, complete,
total, full

**equal**
identical, uniform,
like,
indistinguishable

**essential**
crucial, necessary,
key, vital, needed,
required, requisite,
important

**eternal**
endless, perpetual,
undying, immortal

**even**
flat, smooth,
uniform, featureless,
unbroken,
undamaged

**everyday**
daily, day-to-day

**evident**
obvious, apparent,
noticeable,
conspicuous,
perceptible, visible,
discernible,
transparent, clear

**evil**
wicked, bad, wrong,
wrongful, unholy,
foul, vile, base

**exact**

precise, accurate,
correct, faithful,
close, true, literal,
strict

**excellent**
superb, outstanding,
magnificent,
exceptional,
marvelous,
wonderful, perfect

**exceptional**
unusual,
uncommon,
extraordinary, rare,
singular,
unprecedented,
unexpected,
surprising

**excited**
elevated, animated

**exclusive**
select, chic, elite,
fashionable, stylish,
elegant, special

**excruciating**
severe, acute,
intense, extreme,
savage, violent,
searing, piercing

**exotic**
foreign, tropical

**expansive**
extensive, sweeping,
rolling

**expensive**
costly, dear

**experienced**
skilled,
accomplished,
adept, consummate,
professional

**explosive**
volatile, unstable

**exposed**
unprotected, open

**expressionless**
inscrutable,
unreadable

**exquisite**
beautiful, lovely,
elegant, graceful

**extensive**
large, substantial,
considerable, ample,
great, huge, vast,
immense

**extra**
additional, added,
secondary

**extraordinary**
remarkable,
exceptional,

amazing,
astonishing,
marvelous,
wonderful,
sensational,
stunning, incredible,
unbelievable,
miraculous

**extreme**

utmost, greatest,
maximum, ultimate,
supreme,
paramount, great

# F

**fabulous**
tremendous, prodigious

**faceless**
nondescript, unremarkable

**faint**
indistinct, vague, unclear, obscure, imperceptible

**fair**
just, honest, upright, honorable, trustworthy

**faithful**
loyal, constant, true, devoted, steadfast, dedicated, committed

**fake**
false, bogus

**fallen**
dead, deceased

**false**
wrong, faulty, distorted

**familiar**
known, accustomed

**famous**
celebrated, prominent, famed, popular

**fancy**
elaborate, ornate, decorative, intricate

**fantastic**
extravagant, extraordinary, irrational, wild, mad, absurd, incredible, unbelievable, unthinkable

**far**
distant, faraway

**fascinating**
interesting, enchanting

**fast**
speedy, quick, swift, rapid

**fat**
plump, stout, overweight, heavy, large, solid, chubby, portly

**fatal**

deadly, lethal,
mortal

**fearful**
afraid, frightened,
scared

**fearless**
bold, brave,
courageous, valiant,
gallant, heroic,
daring

**fearsome**
frightening,
terrifying, chilling,
alarming, startling,
unnerving,
daunting,
formidable

**feeble**
weak, weakened,
puny, frail, delicate,
sickly, unwell

**feminine**
girlish, female

**feral**
wild, untrained

**ferocious**
fierce, savage, wild,
feral

**fevered**
feverish, hot

**feverish**

fevered, hot

**few**
scarce, scant,
insufficient

**fierce**
ferocious, savage,
vicious

**filthy**
dirty, grimy, muddy,
murky, slimy

**final**
last, terminal,
ultimate, eventual

**financial**
economic,
commercial

**fine**
excellent, first-class,
great, exceptional,
outstanding,
admirable, superior,
splendid,
magnificent,
beautiful

**firm**
hard, solid,
unyielding, resistant

**fitting**
apt, appropriate,
suitable

**flash**

bold, flamboyant,
conspicuous,
extravagant,
expensive,
pretentious

**flat**
level, horizontal

**flawless**
perfect, unmarked

**fleeting**
brief, short-lived,
short, momentary,
sudden, cursory,
fading

**flimsy**
insubstantial, slight,
light, fragile, frail,
shaky, unstable,
wobbly, rickety,
ramshackle

**fluorescent**
bright, ablaze,
brilliant, glowing,
sparkling

**foolish**
stupid, silly, idiotic,
witless, mindless,
irresponsible

**foreign**
distant, remote,
external, outside

**formal**
ceremonial, ritual,
conventional,
traditional

**formidable**
intimidating,
daunting, alarming,
frightening,
terrifying, chilling,
disturbing

**forthcoming**
imminent,
impending, near

**fortunate**
lucky, blessed,
happy

**foul**
disgusting, repulsive,
offensive, awful,
dreadful, horrible

**fragile**
brittle, flimsy, weak,
frail, insubstantial,
delicate, dainty

**frail**
weak, weakened,
feeble, crippled

**frank**
direct, plain,
straight,

straightforward,
explicit
**frantic**
panicky, distraught,
distressed
**frenzied**
frantic, wild,
fraught, feverish,
fevered, mad,
crazed, manic,
energetic
**frequent**
repeated, persistent,
continuing,
constant, incessant
**fresh**
crisp, firm
**friendly**
affectionate,
amiable, cordial,
warm
**frightened**
anxious, disturbed,
troubled, distressed,
concerned, upset,
distraught, uneasy
**frightening**
terrifying, alarming,
startling, shocking,
chilling, appalling,
disturbing

**frigid**
bitter, frozen, frosty,
icy, ice-cold, chilly,
wintry, bleak
**frozen**
ice-cold, icy, frosted
**frustrated**
upset, downcast,
depressed, dismayed
**full-time**
professional,
permanent,
committed
**funny**
amusing, humorous,
comic, comical
**furious**
enraged,
incandescent,
boiling, seething,
frenzied
**furtive**
secretive, secret
**futile**
fruitless, vain,
pointless
**future**
subsequent,
upcoming
**fuzzy**

velvety, silky, silken,
soft

# G

**gaunt**
haggard, skeletal,
skinny, spindly,
thin, spare

**general**
widespread,
common, extensive,
universal, wide,
popular, public

**generous**
liberal, lavish

**genetic**
inherent, innate

**gentle**
kind, kindly, tender,
benign, merciful,
sympathetic

**genuine**
authentic, real,
actual, original, true,
veritable

**ghastly**
terrible, horrible,
grim, awful, dire

**ghostly**
spectral, phantom,
unearthly,

unnatural,
supernatural,
insubstantial

**giant**
huge, colossal,
massive, enormous,
gigantic, great,
mammoth, vast,
immense,
tremendous

**giddy**
dizzy, light-headed,
faint, weak,
unsteady, shaky,
wobbly

**gifted**
talented, skilled,
accomplished,
consummate,
polished

**gigantic**
huge, enormous,
vast, extensive,
expansive, broad,
wide

**glad**
pleased, happy,
delighted, gleeful

**glaring**
dazzling, strong,
harsh

**glassy**
  smooth, shiny, glossy, polished

**global**
  worldwide, international

**gloomy**
  dark, shadowy, dim, dingy, drab, dismal, dreary

**glorious**
  celebrated, famous, famed, renowned, distinguished, excellent, outstanding, great

**glossy**
  shiny, bright, brilliant, sparkling, sleek, silky, silken

**glowing**
  bright, radiant, incandescent, luminous

**gnarled**
  knotted, lumpy, bumpy, rough

**golden**
  blonde, yellow, yellowish, fair

**good-looking**
  attractive, beautiful, pretty, handsome, lovely, stunning, striking, arresting, gorgeous

**good**
  fine, superior

**gorgeous**
  good-looking, attractive, handsome, lovely, beautiful, pretty, stunning, striking, arresting

**graceful**
  elegant, stylish, refined, sophisticated, dignified, distinguished

**gracious**
  courteous, polite, civil, civilized, diplomatic

**grand**
  magnificent, imposing, impressive, splendid, resplendent, superb, striking,

monumental,
majestic, glorious

**grassy**
green, leafy

**grateful**
thankful,
appreciative

**grave**
serious, important,
profound,
significant,
momentous,
weighty

**greasy**
oily, fat

**great**
considerable,
substantial,
pronounced,
significant, serious,
exceptional,
extraordinary,
special

**greedy**
ravenous, insatiable

**grim**
stern, aloof, distant

**grimy**
dirty, grubby, filthy,
messy

**grisly**
gruesome, ghastly,
horrid, fearful,
hideous, macabre,
horrible, grim

**gross**
overweight, fat, big,
large, massive,
immense, huge,
colossal

**grotesque**
misshapen,
distorted, twisted,
gnarled

**gruesome**
grisly, ghastly,
horrid, fearful,
hideous, macabre,
horrible, grim

**gruff**
abrupt, brusque,
curt, short, blunt,
no-nonsense

**guilty**
responsible,
accountable, liable

**guttural**
throaty, husky,
gruff, gravelly,
harsh, rough,
rasping

# H

**hairy**
shaggy, bushy

**halfway**
middle, central

**handsome**
good-looking,
attractive, striking,
stunning, fine

**handy**
useful, convenient,
practical, helpful,
functional

**happy**
contented, content,
cheerful, cheery,
merry, joyful, jovial,
jolly, gleeful,
carefree

**hard**
firm, solid, dense,
rigid, stiff, resistant,
unbreakable,
impenetrable,
unyielding

**hardened**
accustomed, used

**harmless**
safe, innocuous,
benign, gentle, mild,
wholesome

**harsh**
jarring, rasping,
raspy, raucous,
metallic

**hasty**
quick, hurried, fast,
swift, rapid, speedy,
brisk

**hateful**
horrible, horrid,
unpleasant, awful,
nasty, rotten

**hazy**
misty, foggy, cloudy,
clouded, murky,
overcast

**healthy**
fine, fit

**hearty**
exuberant, cheerful,
jovial, lively, loud,
animated

**heavy**
weighty, hefty, big,
large, substantial,
massive, ponderous

**helpful**

friendly, pleasant,
kind, thoughtful,
supportive,
cooperative,
sympathetic

**helpless**
dependent,
incapable,
powerless,
impotent, weak,
feeble

**heroic**
brave, courageous,
valiant, bold, daring,
superhuman,
fearless

**hesitant**
uncertain, unsure,
doubtful, dubious,
tentative, reluctant,
nervous

**hidden**
secret, invisible,
unseen, masked

**hideous**
ugly, repulsive,
gruesome,
disgusting,
grotesque,
monstrous, grim,
ghastly, macabre

**high-pitched**
high, shrill, acute,
sharp, piercing,
penetrating

**high**
tall, lofty, towering,
elevated, giant, big

**hind**
back, rear

**hip**
fashionable, popular

**historical**
recorded, authentic,
actual, true

**hoarse**
rough, harsh,
throaty, gruff,
husky, guttural,
gravelly, cracked

**hollow**
empty, vacant

**holy**
pious, religious,
devout, spiritual

**honest**
upright, honorable,
moral, ethical,
righteous,
respectable

**hopeful**

optimistic, confident, positive, cheerful, expectant

**hopeless**
desperate, downcast, wretched

**horrible**
dreadful, horrific, fearful, awful, terrible, shocking, appalling, hideous, grim

**horrific**
dreadful, horrible, awful, terrible, fearful, shocking, appalling, hideous

**hostile**
aggressive, belligerent

**hot**
heated, sizzling, boiling, searing, red-hot

**huge**
enormous, vast, immense, great, massive, cosmic, colossal, prodigious, gigantic

**humble**
meek, respectful, submissive

**humid**
close, sultry, sticky, steamy, oppressive, airless, stuffy, clammy

**hungry**
ravenous, empty, hollow

**hurried**
quick, fast, swift, rapid, speedy, brisk, hasty

**husky**
throaty, gruff, deep, gravelly, hoarse, coarse, rough, thick, guttural

**hysterical**
emotional, uncontrollable, frenzied, frantic, wild, feverish

# I

**iced**
cool, cold

**icy**
frozen, frosty, frosted, glassy, slippery

**ideal**
perfect, consummate, supreme, absolute, complete, flawless, classic

**identical**
similar, indistinguishable, uniform, twin

**idle**
lazy, inert, sluggish, listless

**ill**
unwell, sick, sickly

**illegal**
illicit, illegitimate, criminal

**imaginary**
unreal, fictional, fictitious, pretend, mythical, legendary, fantastic

**immediate**
instant, instantaneous, prompt, swift, speedy, rapid, quick

**immense**
huge, vast, massive, enormous, gigantic, colossal, cosmic, great, extensive, expansive

**imminent**
impending, close, near, forthcoming

**immortal**
undying, eternal, endless, perpetual, lasting, enduring, constant

**impassive**
expressionless, inscrutable, blank

**impatient**
restless, nervous, anxious, edgy, jumpy, jittery

**impending**
imminent, close,

near, forthcoming, upcoming

**impenetrable**
impervious, solid, dense, thick, hard, unyielding, unbreakable, resistant

**important**
significant, momentous, major

**impressive**
magnificent, majestic, imposing, splendid, spectacular, grand, stunning, breathtaking

**incapable**
incompetent, inadequate

**incredible**
unbelievable, strained, improbable

**incredulous**
doubtful, dubious, unconvinced

**individual**
single, separate, independent

**inevitable**
unavoidable, inescapable, inexorable, certain, sure

**infinite**
unlimited, limitless, interminable, cosmic

**inhuman**
cruel, harsh, brutal, callous, sadistic, severe, savage, vicious, barbaric

**injured**
wounded, sore, damaged, disabled

**inky**
black, jet-black, pitch-black, ebony, dark

**inner**
central, middle, interior, nuclear

**inside**
inner, interior, internal, inmost

**insignificant**
unimportant, trivial

**insistent**
persistent, determined,

adamant, tenacious,
unyielding,
unrelenting,
inexorable

**instant**
immediate,
instantaneous,
prompt, direct,
swift, speedy, rapid,
quick, express

**intact**
whole, entire,
complete,
unbroken,
undamaged,
unharmed,
uninjured, flawless,
unscathed

**intelligent**
clever, bright,
brilliant, sharp,
quick, smart,
thinking

**intense**
great, acute,
enormous, fierce,
severe, extreme,
high, exceptional,
extraordinary,
harsh, strong,
powerful

**intent**
bent, determined,
insistent, keen

**interested**
attentive, intent,
focused, rapt

**interesting**
fascinating,
gripping,
compelling

**interior**
inside, inner,
internal

**internal**
inner, interior,
inside

**international**
global, worldwide

**intimate**
close, dear,
cherished, familiar,
confidential,
faithful, constant,
devoted, fast, firm

**intricate**
complex,
complicated,
tangled, twisted,
serpentine

**intriguing**

interesting,
fascinating,
compelling,
gripping

**ironic**

sarcastic, sardonic,
dry, sharp, stinging,
acid, bitter

**irregular**

uneven, crooked,
misshapen, lopsided,
contorted, twisted

**irresistible**

tempting, seductive

**irritated**

annoyed, angry,
disgruntled

**isolated**

remote, secluded,
lonely

# J

**jagged**
spiky, spiked,
barbed, pointed,
ragged, craggy,
rough, uneven,
irregular, broken

**joint**
common, shared,
communal,
collective, corporate

**just**
fair, neutral,
disinterested

**juvenile**
young, teenage,
adolescent, junior,
underage

# K

**keen**
eager, anxious,
impatient,
determined,
ambitious, ready

**key**
crucial, central,
essential, basic,
fundamental,
critical, decisive,
dominant, vital,
principal

**kind**
kindly, good-
natured, tender,
caring, affectionate,
loving

# L

**large**
big, great, huge, substantial, immense, enormous, colossal, massive, mammoth, vast

**lazy**
idle, inert, sluggish, listless

**lean**
slim, thin, slender, spare, wiry, slight

**legal**
legitimate, valid

**legendary**
fabled, heroic, ancient, traditional, romantic, mythical

**lengthy**
long, prolonged, extended, extensive

**lethal**
fatal, deadly, mortal, murderous, terminal, final

**lifeless**
dead, deceased, late, extinct, stiff

**light-headed**
dizzy, giddy, faint, unsteady

**light**
bright, sunny, brilliant

**like**
similar, corresponding, parallel

**likely**
probable, possible, credible, plausible, believable, imaginable

**limited**
finite, little, narrow, tight, lean, slight, slender, short

**limp**
soft, loose, slack, lax

**liquid**
fluid, flowing

**little**
small, compact

**lively**
energetic, active, animated, vigorous,

outgoing, spirited,
enthusiastic, vibrant

**livid**
furious, angry

**loaded**
full, laden, packed,
stuffed

**logical**
rational, sound,
valid

**lone**
solitary, single, solo,
alone, sole

**lonely**
isolated, alone,
abandoned

**long-term**
enduring, lifelong,
continuing,
permanent

**long**
lengthy, extended,
prolonged, extensive

**lost**
missing, forgotten

**loud**
noisy, booming,
thunderous,
thundering

**lousy**
awful, terrible,
appalling, desperate,
unspeakable,
miserable

**lovely**
beautiful, pretty,
attractive, good-
looking, appealing,
handsome, adorable,
exquisite, sweet,
charming

**loving**
affectionate, fond,
devoted

**low**
short, small, little

**loyal**
faithful, true,
devoted

**lucky**
fortunate, blessed

**luminous**
bright, brilliant,
radiant, dazzling,
glowing

**lush**
rich, exuberant,
vigorous

**luxurious**
opulent, sumptuous,
expensive, rich,

costly, lush, grand,
splendid,
magnificent

# M

**mad**
insane, crazy, crazed

**magical**
supernatural, magic, mystical, preternatural, spectral, ghostly, secret, dark

**magnificent**
splendid, spectacular, impressive, striking, glorious, superb, majestic, awesome, breathtaking

**main**
principal, chief, foremost, major, dominant, central, key

**major**
greatest, chief, main, prime, principal

**makeshift**
temporary, impromptu

**many**
numerous, countless, innumerable

**martial**
military, naval

**mass**
universal, widespread, general, extensive

**massive**
huge, enormous, gigantic, great, giant, colossal, mammoth, vast, immense, tremendous

**matter-of-fact**
practical, sensible, realistic, rational, sober, pragmatic, businesslike

**maximum**
greatest, top, topmost, utmost, supreme, paramount, extreme

**meaningful**
significant, relevant, important, weighty, valid, worthwhile, purposeful

**meaningless**

unintelligible,
incomprehensible,
incoherent,
senseless, foolish,
silly, absurd,
ridiculous

**mechanical**
automated,
automatic

**medieval**
gothic, early

**medium**
average, moderate,
fair, normal,
standard, usual

**mental**
intellectual, rational,
psychological,
abstract

**merciless**
ruthless, implacable,
inexorable,
relentless

**mere**
bare, trivial, paltry,
basic, scant,
minimal, slender

**merry**
cheerful, cheery,
bright, sunny, lively,
carefree

**messy**
dirty, filthy, grubby,
grimy

**middle**
central, mean,
medium, halfway

**mighty**
powerful, forceful,
violent, ferocious,
fierce, brutal,
vicious, vigorous,
hefty, thunderous,
savage, destructive

**mild**
gentle, tender, soft,
sensitive,
sympathetic, warm,
unassuming, placid

**military**
armed, martial

**milky**
pale, white, creamy,
pearly, ivory

**mindless**
stupid, idiotic,
witless, foolish

**minor**
slight, small

**miraculous**
supernatural,
preternatural,

superhuman,
inexplicable,
fantastic, magical,
prodigious

**miserable**
unhappy, sad,
sorrowful,
depressed,
downcast, down

**misshapen**
distorted, crooked,
contorted, wry,
twisted, bent

**missing**
lost, absent

**misty**
hazy, foggy, cloudy,
steamy, murky,
smoky

**mixed**
assorted, varied,
different, diverse,
motley

**mock**
artificial, man-made,
synthetic, plastic, so-
called, fake, false

**modern**
contemporary,
present, current,
recent

**modest**
humble,
unassuming

**moist**
damp, steamy,
humid, clammy,
dank, wet, rainy

**molten**
liquid, fluid,
flowing, soft

**momentary**
brief, short, short-
lived, quick, fleeting,
temporary

**monstrous**
grotesque, hideous,
ugly, ghastly,
gruesome, horrible,
horrid, horrific,
grisly, disgusting

**mortal**
physical, bodily,
corporal, earthly

**motionless**
still, stationary,
immobile,
immovable, static

**mournful**
sad, sorrowful,
melancholy,

miserable, unhappy,
heartbroken

**muddy**
slimy, sodden

**multiple**
numerous, many,
various, different,
diverse, several,
compound

**mundane**
dull, boring, tedious,
monotonous,
tiresome

**murderous**
brutal, violent,
savage, ferocious,
fierce, vicious,
bloodthirsty,
barbaric, cruel,
inhuman

**murky**
dark, gloomy, gray,
leaden, dull, dim,
overcast, cloudy,
clouded, foggy,
misty

**musical**
sweet, liquid

**musty**
stale, damp, dank,
smelly, stuffy, airless

**mute**
silent, speechless,
dumb, wordless,
tight-lipped

**muted**
faint, indistinct,
quiet, soft, low, dull

**mysterious**
puzzling, strange,
peculiar, curious,
funny, queer, odd,
weird, bizarre,
inexplicable

**mystical**
spiritual, religious,
supernatural,
preternatural

# N

**naked**
nude, bare

**nameless**
unnamed,
unidentified,
anonymous

**nasty**
unpleasant,
disgusting,
distasteful, awful,
dreadful, horrible,
terrible, vile, foul

**national**
public, federal

**native**
indigenous, original,
first

**natural**
normal, ordinary,
everyday, usual,
regular, common,
typical, routine,
standard, customary

**near**
close, nearby,
accessible, handy

**nearby**
close, near, adjacent

**neat**
tidy, orderly,
immaculate

**necessary**
obligatory, requisite,
required,
mandatory,
imperative, needed

**nervous**
anxious, edgy, tense,
jumpy, skittish,
brittle, hysterical

**net**
clear, final

**neutral**
disinterested, fair

**new**
current, state-of-
the-art,
contemporary,
advanced, recent

**nice**
enjoyable, pleasant,
pleasurable,
agreeable, delightful,
satisfying,
acceptable,
entertaining,
amusing

**noisy**

rowdy, boisterous,
turbulent

**normal**
usual, standard,
typical, common,
ordinary, customary,
conventional,
accustomed

**nude**
naked, bare

**numb**
dead, senseless

**numerous**
many, countless,
innumerable

# O

**oblivious**
unaware, unconscious, heedless, ignorant, blind, deaf, unsuspecting

**obvious**
clear, plain, evident, apparent, conspicuous, pronounced, transparent

**occasional**
intermittent, irregular, odd, random, casual, uncommon

**odd**
strange, peculiar, weird, queer, funny, bizarre, eccentric, unusual, unconventional

**offensive**
insulting, rude, disrespectful, abusive

**official**
authentic, formal

**ok**
satisfactory, fine, acceptable, competent

**old**
elderly, mature, senior

**olive**
sallow, dusky, black, ebony

**ominous**
threatening, baleful, sinister, dire

**ongoing**
continuing, current

**opaque**
cloudy, filmy, hazy, misty, dirty, dingy, muddy, grimy

**optimistic**
cheerful, cheery, positive, confident, hopeful, bright

**orderly**
neat, tidy, trim, straight

**ordinary**
usual, normal, standard, typical,

common,
customary,
accustomed,
everyday

**organized**
orderly, efficient,
neat, tidy,
methodical,
businesslike,
planned

**original**
indigenous, native

**ornate**
elaborate, fancy,
busy

**other**
alternative,
different, distinct,
separate

**outdoor**
outside, exterior,
external

**outer**
outside, outward,
exterior, external,
superficial

**outrageous**
shocking, appalling,
monstrous, heinous

**outside**
exterior, external,
outer, outward,
outdoor

**overall**
general, universal,
gross, net, final

**overhead**
aerial, elevated

**overnight**
quick, fast, swift,
speedy, express,
brisk, lively, prompt,
fleeting

**oversized**
large, substantial,
considerable, great,
huge, immense,
enormous,
extensive, colossal,
massive

**overwhelming**
enormous,
immense, massive,
huge, formidable,
prodigious,
fantastic, staggering

# P

**packed**
 crowded, full,
 loaded, solid

**pained**
 upset, wounded,
 injured, distressed,
 disgruntled

**painful**
 sore, tender,
 excruciating

**pale**
 white, pallid, wan,
 bloodless, ashen

**palpable**
 tangible, noticeable,
 solid, concrete,
 substantial, real

**paranoid**
 suspicious, fearful,
 insecure

**partial**
 incomplete, limited,
 unfinished

**particular**
 specific, certain,
 distinct, separate,
 isolated

**passionate**
 intense, fervent,
 fiery, heated,
 feverish, emotional,
 heartfelt

**past**
 finished, forgotten,
 former

**pathetic**
 pitiful, touching,
 poignant, plaintive

**peaceful**
 tranquil, calm,
 pleasant, quiet, still,
 soothing, sleepy,
 silent, soundless

**peculiar**
 strange, unusual,
 odd, funny, curious,
 bizarre, weird,
 uncanny, queer,
 unexpected,
 unfamiliar

**perfect**
 ideal, flawless,
 consummate,
 ultimate

**perilous**
 dangerous, risky,
 treacherous

**permanent**

lasting, enduring,
continuing,
perpetual, eternal,
constant, persistent

**persistent**
tenacious,
determined,
resolute, purposeful,
single-minded,
tireless, patient,
diligent

**personal**
distinctive,
characteristic,
unique, individual,
particular, private,
peculiar, exclusive

**pet**
tame, domestic

**petite**
small, dainty,
diminutive, slight,
little, tiny, delicate

**petty**
trivial, minor, small,
slight, unimportant,
insignificant, paltry

**physical**
bodily, corporal

**piercing**
shrill, high-pitched,
penetrating, loud,
strong

**pitiful**
sad, pathetic,
disturbing,
heartbreaking

**plain**
obvious, clear,
evident, apparent,
visible, discernible,
perceptible

**plastic**
flexible, soft, supple

**plausible**
credible, reasonable,
believable, likely,
probable, possible,
imaginable,
convincing

**playful**
jolly, lively, spirited,
exuberant, perky,
skittish

**pleasant**
enjoyable, pleasing,
pleasurable, nice,
agreeable, satisfying,
welcome, good,
acceptable

**pleased**

happy, glad,
delighted, grateful,
thankful, content,
contented, satisfied

**plump**
chubby, fat, stout,
ample, round

**plush**
luxurious,
sumptuous, lavish,
gorgeous, opulent,
splendid,
magnificent, lush

**pointed**
sharp, acute

**pointless**
senseless, futile,
hopeless, fruitless,
useless, needless, idle

**poisonous**
venomous, deadly

**polished**
shiny, bright, glossy

**polite**
civil, courteous,
respectful, gallant

**political**
diplomatic,
constitutional,
public

**positive**

good, enthusiastic,
supportive,
reassuring,
encouraging

**possible**
viable, manageable

**potent**
powerful, strong,
vigorous, mighty,
formidable,
influential,
commanding,
dominant, forceful,
overpowering

**potential**
possible, likely,
prospective, future,
probable, budding

**powerful**
strong, muscular,
sturdy, robust,
mighty, hefty, burly,
husky, athletic

**powerless**
impotent, helpless,
inadequate, useless,
vulnerable, weak,
feeble

**practical**
pragmatic, real,

actual, active,
experimental

**precious**
valuable, costly,
expensive, dear

**precise**
exact, accurate,
correct, specific,
detailed, explicit,
meticulous, close

**preliminary**
initial, prior

**present**
near, nearby,
adjacent, available,
ready

**pretend**
imaginary, made-up,
unreal

**pretty**
attractive, lovely,
good-looking,
appealing,
charming,
delightful, nice,
pleasing

**primal**
basic, fundamental,
essential, elemental,
primary, vital,
central, inherent

**primary**
main, chief, key,
prime, central,
principal, foremost,
first, paramount

**prime**
main, chief, key,
primary, central,
principal, foremost,
first, paramount,
major, dominant

**primitive**
ancient, first,
antique, primal,
primary, original

**prior**
previous,
preliminary, initial

**pristine**
immaculate, perfect,
spotless, flawless,
clean, fresh, new,
virgin

**private**
personal, individual,
particular, special,
exclusive

**profound**
heartfelt, intense,
keen, great, extreme,

sincere, earnest,
deep

**prolonged**
continuous,
ongoing, steady,
continuing,
constant, persistent,
perpetual

**prominent**
important,
distinguished,
notable, public,
outstanding,
foremost

**promising**
good, encouraging,
hopeful, optimistic,
positive, bright, rosy

**prone**
susceptible,
vulnerable, liable,
inclined, subject,
open

**proper**
real, genuine, actual,
true

**proud**
pleased, glad, happy,
delighted

**psychic**
supernatural,
preternatural,
magic, magical,
mystical

**psychological**
mental, emotional,
intellectual, inner,
rational, abstract

**public**
national, federal

**puffy**
swollen, full,
bloated, baggy

**pungent**
strong, powerful

**pure**
solid, refined

**purple**
ornate, fancy,
extravagant, busy

# Q

**queer**
odd, strange,
unusual, funny,
peculiar, curious,
bizarre, weird,
eccentric,
unconventional

**quick**
fast, swift, rapid,
speedy

**quiet**
silent, still,
soundless

# R

**radiant**
bright, brilliant,
glowing, ablaze,
luminous

**ragged**
torn, worn

**rainy**
wet, damp

**random**
casual, stray, erratic

**rapid**
quick, fast, swift,
speedy, express,
brisk, lively, prompt,
fleeting

**rare**
scarce, sparse,
scattered, golden

**rational**
logical, sensible,
reasonable,
coherent,
intelligent, wise

**razor-sharp**
shrewd, sharp,
acute, quick,
ingenious, clever,

intelligent, bright,
brilliant, smart

**ready**
prepared, organized

**reasonable**
sensible, rational,
logical, fair, just,
decent

**recent**
new, late, current,
fresh, modern,
contemporary, latter

**reckless**
careless, heedless,
hasty

**recognizable**
noticeable,
perceptible,
discernible

**red**
scarlet, ruby, cherry

**regular**
uniform, even,
consistent, constant,
orderly

**relative**
respective, parallel,
corresponding

**relentless**
persistent,
continuing,

constant,
continuous, lasting,
steady,
uninterrupted

**reliable**
good, authentic,
definitive, valid,
genuine, sound, true

**relieved**
glad, thankful,
grateful, pleased,
happy

**religious**
devout, pious,
reverent, dutiful,
holy

**reluctant**
unwilling, grudging,
resistant

**remarkable**
extraordinary,
exceptional,
amazing,
astonishing,
marvelous,
wonderful,
sensational,
stunning, incredible,
unbelievable,
miraculous

**remote**

faraway, distant, far

**respectable**
upright, honest,
honorable,
trustworthy,
worthy, decent,
good, admirable

**respectful**
reverent, humble,
dutiful

**restless**
uneasy, edgy, tense,
nervous, anxious

**rhythmic**
measured, repeated

**rich**
wealthy, prosperous,
opulent, substantial

**rickety**
shaky, unsteady,
dilapidated,
ramshackle

**ridiculous**
absurd, comical,
funny, hilarious,
humorous, amusing,
entertaining

**right**
just, fair, good,
upright, righteous,

proper, moral,
ethical, honorable

**righteous**
good, upright,
decent, worthy

**rigid**
stiff, hard, firm,
unyielding

**ripe**
mature, soft, lush,
juicy, tender

**risky**
dangerous, perilous,
insecure, exposed,
precarious, tricky

**rocky**
stony, rough,
bumpy, rugged, hard

**romantic**
intimate, passionate

**rotten**
bad, off, putrid,
spoiled

**rough**
uneven, irregular,
bumpy, stony,
rocky, broken,
rugged, craggy

**rounded**
rich, full, mellow

**routine**
standard, regular,
customary,
accustomed,
normal, usual,
ordinary, natural,
typical

**rude**
insolent,
disrespectful

**rueful**
sorrowful, regretful,
apologetic, sorry,
sheepish, contrite

**rugged**
rough, uneven,
bumpy, rocky,
stony, irregular,
jagged, craggy

**ruthless**
merciless, cruel,
heartless, hard,
stony, cold-blooded,
harsh

# S

**sacred**
holy, hallowed, blessed, dedicated

**sad**
unhappy, sorrowful, regretful, depressed, downcast, miserable, down

**safe**
sheltered, guarded, secure

**sandy**
grainy, gravelly, stony

**sane**
lucid, rational, coherent, balanced

**sarcastic**
sardonic, ironic

**satisfied**
pleased, happy, content, contented

**satisfying**
pleasing, enjoyable, pleasurable

**savage**
ferocious, fierce

**scant**
little, minimal, limited

**scarce**
short, scant, sparse, insufficient

**scared**
frightened, afraid, fearful, nervous, panicky, alarmed, worried

**scarlet**
ruby, cherry

**scary**
frightening, terrifying, chilling, alarming, appalling, daunting

**scrawny**
skinny, thin, gaunt, bony, angular

**searing**
flaming, fiery

**seasoned**
experienced, sophisticated, veteran, hardened

**secondary**
lesser, minor, peripheral

**secret**

confidential,
classified, untold,
unknown

**secretive**
secret, silent, quiet,
tight-lipped, close

**secure**
tight, firm, taut,
secured

**seeming**
apparent, outward

**self-conscious**
embarrassed,
uncomfortable,
uneasy, nervous,
tense, edgy

**senseless**
unconscious, cold,
stunned, numb,
comatose

**sensible**
practical, realistic,
responsible,
reasonable, rational,
logical, sound,
balanced, sober, no-
nonsense

**sensual**
physical, carnal,
bodily, animal

**separate**
unrelated, different,
distinct

**serene**
calm, cool, calm,
tranquil, peaceful

**serious**
solemn, earnest,
grave, sober, stern,
grim, dour

**severe**
acute, serious, grave,
critical, dire, drastic,
grievous, extreme,
dreadful, terrible,
awful

**sexy**
seductive, desirable,
sensual, sultry,
provocative,
tempting

**shabby**
scruffy, dilapidated,
ramshackle

**shadowy**
dark, dim, gloomy,
murky

**shaggy**
hairy, bushy, thick

**shaky**
tremulous,

unsteady, wobbly,
weak
**shallow**
superficial, slight,
flimsy, insubstantial,
lightweight, empty,
trivial
**sharp**
keen, razor-sharp
**shattered**
devastated, shocked,
shell-shocked,
stunned, staggered,
dumbfounded,
crushed
**sheer**
utter, complete,
absolute, total, pure,
perfect, thorough,
consummate
**shiny**
glossy, glassy, bright,
polished, smooth
**shocking**
appalling, horrific,
dreadful, awful,
terrible, horrible,
outrageous, vile
**short**
small, little, tiny,
minuscule

**shrewd**
sharp, acute,
intelligent, clever,
alert, perceptive
**shrill**
high pitched,
piercing, high,
sharp, penetrating,
loud, strong
**shy**
timid, sheepish,
reserved
**sick**
ill, unwell, bad
**sickening**
repulsive, disgusting,
appalling, hideous,
horrible
**significant**
notable, remarkable,
outstanding,
important
**silent**
still, inaudible,
soundless, peaceful,
tranquil
**silken**
thin, light,
lightweight, fine,
sheer, delicate,
insubstantial, filmy

**silky**
smooth, soft, sleek,
fine, glossy, silken,
velvety

**silly**
foolish, stupid,
idiotic, mindless,
witless

**silver**
gray, white, light

**similar**
indistinguishable,
close, near

**simple**
straightforward,
easy, uncomplicated,
effortless, painless,
manageable,
elementary

**sincere**
heartfelt, profound,
deep

**single**
sole, lone, solitary,
isolated

**sinister**
threatening,
ominous, baleful,
frightening, eerie,
alarming,

disturbing, dark,
black

**skeletal**
scrawny, skinny,
bony, angular

**skilled**
experienced,
trained,
professional,
seasoned,
accomplished,
talented

**skinny**
thin, scrawny, bony,
angular, gaunt

**sleek**
smooth, glossy,
shiny, silken, silky,
velvety

**sleepy**
drowsy, tired,
languid

**slender**
slim, lean, willowy,
graceful

**slick**
efficient, smooth,
polished

**slight**
small, modest, little,
tiny, minute,

  imperceptible, insignificant

**slim**
  slender, lean, willowy, graceful, trim, slight

**slimy**
  slippery, greasy, muddy

**slippery**
  greasy, oily, icy, glassy, smooth, slick

**sloppy**
  watery, thin, liquid

**slow**
  unhurried, leisurely, measured, moderate, deliberate, steady, slow-moving, easy

**sluggish**
  listless, lifeless, inert, slow, dull, languid

**sly**
  cunning, crafty, clever, tricky, devious

**small**
  little, compact

**smart**
  fashionable, stylish, chic, elegant, neat, trim

**smoky**
  hazy, foggy, murky, thick

**smooth**
  even, level, flat, flush, featureless

**snowy**
  pristine, immaculate, shiny

**social**
  communal, collective, general, popular, civil, public

**sole**
  only, single, solitary, lone, unique, individual, exclusive, singular

**solemn**
  dignified, ceremonial, stately, courtly, majestic, imposing, impressive, splendid, magnificent

**solid**
  hard, rigid, firm, frozen, concrete

**solitary**
lonely, alone

**soothing**
quiet, calm, calming, reassuring, tranquil, peaceful, placid

**sore**
painful, stinging, irritated

**sorry**
sad, unhappy, sorrowful, distressed, upset, depressed, downcast, miserable, down

**sound**
healthy, fit, undamaged, uninjured

**sour**
acid, bitter, sharp, pungent, acrid, biting

**spacious**
generous, large, big, vast, immense, ample

**spare**
extra, additional, second, alternative, backup

**sparkling**
bright, brilliant

**sparse**
scant, scattered, scarce

**special**
exceptional, particular, unusual, marked, singular, uncommon, notable, remarkable, outstanding, unique

**specific**
particular, certain, determined, distinct, separate, definite, single, individual, peculiar

**spectacular**
impressive, magnificent, splendid, dazzling, sensational, stunning, dramatic, remarkable, outstanding, memorable

**spiritual**

inner, psychic,
psychological

**splendid**
magnificent,
sumptuous, grand,
impressive,
imposing, superb,
spectacular,
resplendent,
opulent, luxurious

**squat**
stocky, stubby,
short, sturdy,
chunky, solid

**stable**
firm, solid, steady,
secure, strong, fast,
stout, sturdy, safe

**stale**
dry, hard, hardened,
old

**standard**
normal, usual,
typical, common,
ordinary, customary,
conventional,
accustomed

**stark**
sharp, crisp, distinct,
obvious, evident,

clear, graphic,
striking

**startling**
surprising,
astonishing,
amazing,
unexpected,
staggering, shocking,
stunning

**static**
unchanged, stable,
steady, constant,
consistent, uniform

**steady**
stable, balanced,
firm, secure,
secured, fast, safe,
immovable

**steep**
sheer, abrupt, sharp,
vertical, dizzy

**stern**
serious, severe, grim,
unfriendly, grave,
sober, austere

**stiff**
rigid, hard, firm,
hardened

**still**
motionless,

immobile,
stationary

**stinking**
fetid, pungent,
acrid, rank, putrid,
noxious

**stony**
rocky, gravelly,
gritty

**stout**
fat, plump, portly,
round, chunky,
overweight

**straightforward**
uncomplicated,
simple, easy,
effortless, painless

**strained**
awkward, tense,
uneasy,
uncomfortable,
fraught, edgy,
difficult, troubled,
embarrassed

**strange**
unusual, odd,
curious, peculiar,
funny, bizarre,
weird, uncanny,
queer, unexpected,
unfamiliar

**stray**
homeless, lost

**stricken**
troubled, injured,
wounded

**strict**
precise, exact, literal,
close, faithful, true,
accurate, careful,
meticulous

**striking**
noticeable, obvious,
conspicuous,
evident, visible,
distinct, prominent,
marked, notable

**strong**
powerful, muscular,
sturdy, hefty, burly,
meaty, robust, fit

**stubborn**
awkward, difficult

**stunning**
remarkable,
extraordinary,
staggering,
incredible,
impressive,
outstanding,
amazing,
astonishing,

marvelous, splendid,
imposing

**stupid**
ignorant, dense,
mindless, foolish,
dull, witless, slow

**sturdy**
muscular, athletic,
strong, hefty,
powerful, solid

**subsequent**
successive, future,
upcoming, next

**substantial**
real, true, actual,
existing

**subtle**
muted, subdued

**successful**
victorious,
triumphant

**sufficient**
enough, adequate,
ample

**suicidal**
hopeless, desperate,
distressed,
heartbroken

**suitable**

acceptable,
satisfactory, fit,
worthy, fitting

**sullen**
surly, sour, resentful,
glum, moody,
gloomy

**sunken**
hollow, depressed,
haggard

**sunny**
bright, sunlit,
brilliant, clear, fine,
fair

**super**
excellent, superb,
first-class, superior,
outstanding,
remarkable,
dazzling, marvelous,
magnificent,
wonderful

**superb**
excellent, first-class,
superior, supreme,
outstanding,
remarkable,
dazzling, marvelous,
magnificent,
wonderful

**superior**

senior, upper
**supernatural**
psychic, magic,
magical, mystical,
miraculous,
superhuman
**sure**
certain, positive,
convinced, definite,
confident, secure,
satisfied
**surprised**
amazed, stunned,
staggered, shocked,
shell-shocked
**surprising**
unexpected,
unpredictable
**surreal**
eccentric, ridiculous,
crazy, absurd, insane
**suspicious**
doubtful, unsure,
dubious, wary,
apprehensive,
cynical
**sweaty**
clammy, sticky,
glowing, moist,
damp, slimy, soggy
**sweeping**
extensive, global,
broad, wide,
worldwide, catholic
**swift**
prompt, rapid,
sudden, immediate,
instant,
instantaneous, ready
**swollen**
bloated, puffy
**sympathetic**
comforting,
supportive,
encouraging

# T

**tactical**
calculated, planned, prudent, strategic, diplomatic, shrewd, clever

**talented**
gifted, skilled, accomplished, brilliant, consummate, polished, artistic

**tall**
big, high, large, huge, towering

**tangled**
twisted, knotted, matted

**taut**
tight, rigid

**technical**
practical, scientific

**tedious**
boring, monotonous, dull, mindless

**teenage**
adolescent, youthful, young, juvenile

**tempting**
attractive, appealing, seductive

**tense**
taut, tight, rigid, strained, stiff

**tentative**
unsettled, preliminary

**terrible**
dreadful, awful, appalling, horrific, horrible, fearful

**terrific**
tremendous, huge, massive, gigantic, colossal, mighty, great, prodigious, formidable

**thankful**
relieved, pleased, glad, grateful

**thick**
wide, broad, deep

**thin**
narrow, fine

**thorough**

minute, detailed,
close, meticulous

**thoughtful**
pensive, thinking,
reflective,
philosophical

**threatening**
intimidating,
frightening,
terrifying, scary,
fearsome, alarming,
baleful

**thunderous**
booming,
resounding, vibrant

**tidy**
neat, orderly,
immaculate

**tight**
firm, fast, secure

**tiny**
minute, mini, toy,
petite, miniature

**tired**
weary, sleepy,
drowsy

**top**
topmost, upper

**torn**
separated, cracked

**total**
entire, complete,
whole, full,
combined, gross,
overall

**tough**
strong, resilient,
resistant, sturdy,
rugged, firm, solid,
substantial, sound,
stout

**towering**
high, tall, lofty,
elevated, steep,
mountainous,
imposing

**traditional**
conventional,
customary,
standard, regular,
normal,
conservative

**tragic**
disastrous,
catastrophic,
devastating, terrible,
dreadful, appalling,
dire, gruesome

**translucent**
glassy, clear,
crystalline,
transparent

**transparent**
clear, translucent,
crystalline, glassy,
liquid

**tremendous**
huge, enormous,
immense, colossal,
massive, prodigious,
monumental,
mammoth, vast,
gigantic

**tricky**
difficult, awkward,
problematic,
delicate, sensitive,
touchy, risky,
uncertain,
precarious

**triumphant**
victorious,
successful, winning

**troubled**
anxious, worried,
concerned,
disturbed, uneasy,
unsettled

**true**
accurate, correct,
faithful, literal

**twisted**
crumpled, crushed,
misshapen,
distorted

# U

**ugly**
hideous, plain

**ultimate**
eventual, last, final,
terminal

**unable**
powerless,
impotent,
inadequate,
incompetent

**unaware**
ignorant,
unconscious,
heedless, oblivious,
unsuspecting,
innocent

**unbearable**
intolerable,
unacceptable,
impossible

**unbelievable**
incredible,
inconceivable,
unthinkable,
unimaginable

**unblinking**
resolute,
determined, single-
minded, firm,
persistent,
committed

**unbroken**
undamaged,
unharmed,
unscathed,
untouched, sound,
intact, whole,
complete, entire

**uncanny**
eerie, unnatural,
preternatural,
supernatural,
unearthly, unreal,
ghostly, mysterious,
strange, odd

**uncertain**
unknown,
unsettled, unsure

**uncomfortable**
painful, intolerable,
unbearable,
excruciating,
cramped

**uncommon**
unusual, rare,
unconventional,
unexpected,

unfamiliar, strange,
odd, curious

**unconscious**
senseless, comatose,
inert

**undercover**
covert, secret,
clandestine, private,
confidential,
conspiratorial,
underground,
furtive

**underground**
subterranean,
sunken

**understandable**
lucid, coherent,
clear, explicit

**uneasy**
worried, anxious,
troubled, disturbed,
nervous, tense, edgy

**uneven**
bumpy, rough,
lumpy, stony, rocky,
jagged

**unfamiliar**
unknown, new,
strange, queer,
foreign, alien

**unfortunate**

unlucky, hapless,
wretched, miserable,
forlorn, unhappy,
poor, pitiful

**unhappy**
sad, miserable,
sorrowful, regretful,
heartbroken, down,
downcast

**unharmed**
uninjured, unhurt,
unscathed, safe, fine

**uniform**
constant, consistent,
steady, stable, static

**unique**
distinctive,
individual, special,
eccentric, isolated

**universal**
general, common

**unknown**
untold, secret,
mysterious, dark,
hidden

**unlikely**
improbable,
doubtful, dubious,
unexpected

**unmistakable**
distinctive, distinct

**unnatural**
  unusual,
  uncommon,
  extraordinary,
  strange, queer, odd,
  peculiar, weird

**unnecessary**
  needless, useless,
  unwanted

**unnoticed**
  unremarkable,
  modest,
  unassuming,
  discreet, hidden

**unpleasant**
  troublesome,
  uncomfortable,
  nasty, horrible,
  appalling

**unpredictable**
  uncertain, unsure,
  doubtful, dubious,
  random

**unseen**
  hidden, invisible,
  imperceptible,
  unnoticed

**unspoken**
  mute, silent

**unstable**
  unsteady, rocky,
  wobbly, rickety,
  shaky

**unsteady**
  unstable, rocky,
  wobbly, rickety,
  shaky

**unusual**
  uncommon,
  unexpected,
  surprising,
  unfamiliar, different

**unwanted**
  unwelcome,
  unfortunate,
  unlucky

**unwelcome**
  unwanted,
  uninvited, unbidden

**unwilling**
  reluctant, hesitant,
  afraid, resistant,
  grudging,
  involuntary

**unyielding**
  stiff, firm, hard,
  solid, tough, tight,
  taut

**upright**
  vertical, straight,
  erect, rampant

**upset**
distressed, troubled,
disturbed, unsettled,
dismayed, worried

**urgent**
acute, grave,
pressing, dire,
desperate, critical,
crucial, sore, serious,
intense, crying

**useful**
functional, practical,
handy, neat,
convenient, helpful

**useless**
futile, pointless,
vain, hopeless

**usual**
customary,
accustomed,
normal, routine,
regular, constant,
standard, typical

**utter**
complete, total,
absolute, thorough,
perfect, outright, all-
out, sheer, positive

# V

**vacant**
empty, unoccupied,
free, available,
unused

**vague**
indistinct, unclear

**valid**
sound, reasonable,
rational, logical

**valuable**
precious, costly,
expensive, dear,
priceless

**various**
diverse, different,
varied, assorted,
mixed

**vast**
huge, extensive,
expansive, broad,
wide, limitless,
infinite, enormous,
gigantic

**verbal**
oral, vocal

**vertical**
upright, erect,
straight

**very**
exact, actual, precise,
particular, specific,
distinct

**vibrant**
resounding,
booming

**vicious**
brutal, ferocious,
savage, violent,
dangerous, ruthless,
merciless, heartless,
callous, cruel, harsh

**vile**
foul, nasty,
unpleasant, bad,
horrid, horrible,
dreadful, offensive,
obnoxious

**violent**
brutal, vicious,
savage, harsh, rough,
aggressive,
threatening, fierce,
wild

**virtual**
effective, near,
essential, practical

**visible**

perceptible,
noticeable,
discernible,
recognizable
## vital
essential, crucial,
key, necessary,
needed, required,
requisite, important
## vivid
bright, brilliant,
glowing, radiant,
vibrant, strong,
bold, deep, intense
## vulnerable
unprotected,
unguarded

# 

**wary**
cautious, careful,
alert, prudent

**watchful**
alert, vigilant,
attentive, perceptive

**watery**
liquid, fluid

**weak**
frail, feeble, puny,
fragile, delicate

**wealthy**
rich, prosperous,
comfortable,
opulent

**weary**
tired, sleepy, drowsy

**weird**
uncanny, eerie,
unnatural,
preternatural,
supernatural,
unearthly, unreal,
ghostly, mysterious,
strange

**welcome**
wanted, popular,
desirable, acceptable

**wet**
damp, moist

**white-hot**
red-hot, fiery, ablaze

**whole**
entire, complete,
full, total

**wicked**
evil, wrong,
wrongful, bad,
corrupt, unholy

**wide**
broad, extensive,
spacious, open, vast

**willing**
ready, prepared,
inclined

**wiry**
sinewy, strong,
tough, athletic

**wise**
intelligent, clever,
enlightened

**wobbly**
unsteady, unstable,
shaky, rocky, rickety

**wonderful**
marvelous,
magnificent, superb,

glorious, lovely,
delightful, first-class

**worn**
shabby, threadbare

**worried**
anxious, disturbed,
troubled, distressed,
concerned, upset,
distraught, uneasy

**worthy**
good, moral, ethical,
noble, upright,
righteous

**wretched**
miserable, unhappy,
sad, heartbroken,
sorrowful, distressed

**wry**
ironic, sardonic,
derisive, sarcastic,
dry

# Y

**yellow**
yellowish, lemon,
amber, gold, golden

**young**
youthful, juvenile